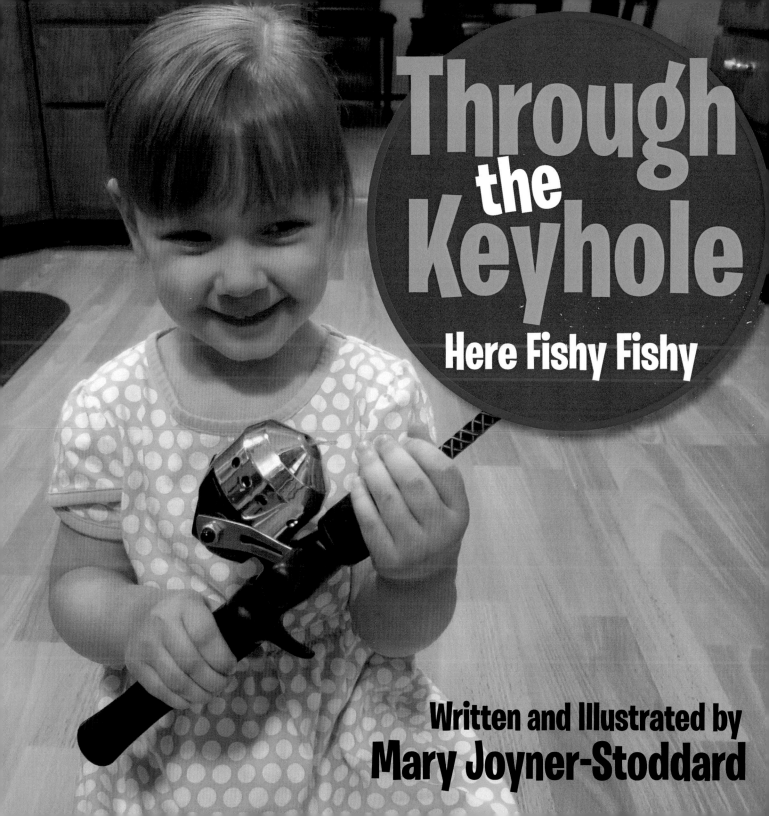

Through the Keyhole
Here Fishy Fishy

Written and Illustrated by
Mary Joyner-Stoddard

Print information available on the last page

Rev. date: 08/27/2015

To order additional copies of this book, contact:
Xlibris
1-888-795-4274
www.Xlibris.com
Orders@Xlibris.com

Through the Keyhole

Here Fishy Fishy

1

"Here Fishy Fishy"

Once I went fishing with
Grandpa and Dad.

I used the best pole a kid ever had.

3

I got it for my birthday this year,

Along with some bobbers
and more fishing gear.

4

5

Grandpa took an old pole,
and fixed it you see.

It was really long; longer than me.

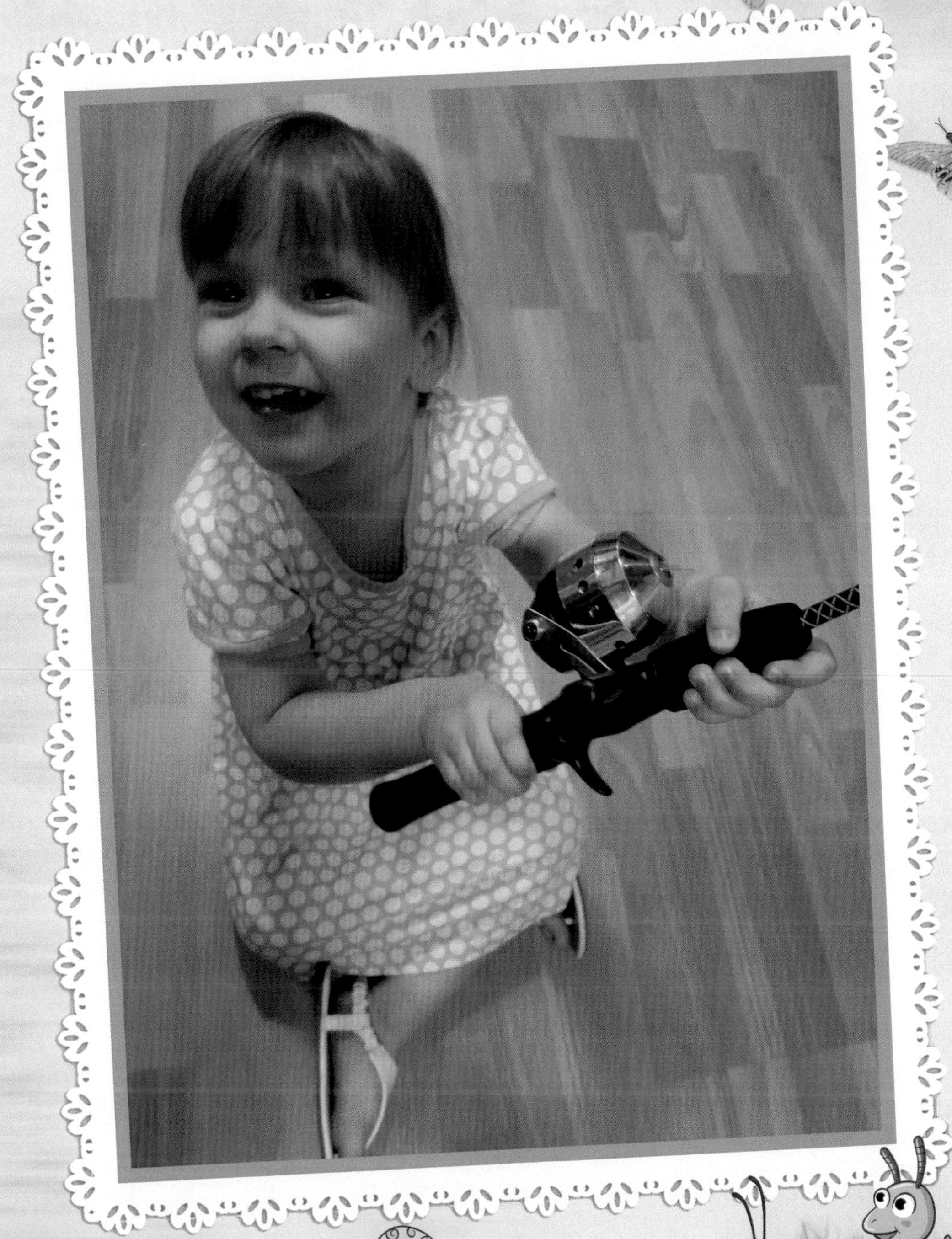

A line of string was tied to the end.

For the hook he used a
nail with a bend.

9

My Dad gave me a vest
and cool fishing hat,

And some plastic worms
that were long and fat.

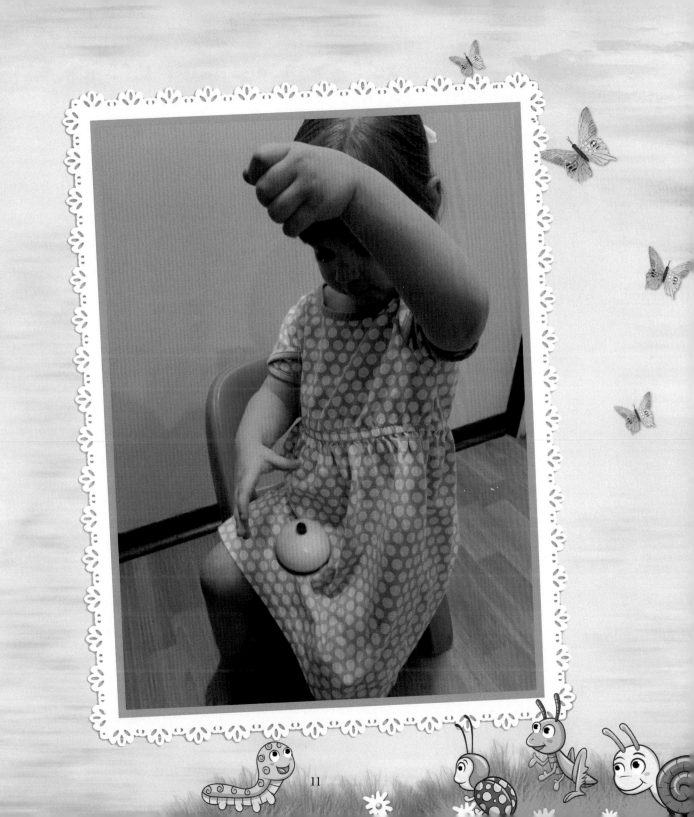

I was hand in hand with Grandpa,
as we walked to the fishing hole.

A smile never left my face, as I
carried my brand new pole.

I threw my line out, just as
proud as could be.

And with a kind voice called,
"here fishy fishy."

13

The grownups laughed at
a little girl's wish.

When all I wanted was to catch a fish.

14

15

A man down the way
heard my sweet call.

And brought me some
fish, stringer and all.

17

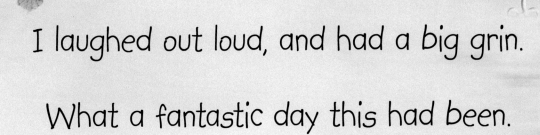

I laughed out loud, and had a big grin.

What a fantastic day this had been.

In my room there's a picture
of me with my fish.

Recording the day I was
granted my wish.

19

We always smile, when
we talk of the day,

A girl caught some fish,
and did it her way.

21

Printed in the United States
By Bookmasters